Kim Porter

Kimberly Antwinette Porter: A Life in Light and Shadow

Kimberly Antwinette Porter was born on December 15, 1970, in Columbus, Georgia. From an early age, she exhibited a flair for the spotlight, beginning her modeling career as a teenager. A proud debutante, Kimberly graduated from Columbus High School in 1988 and soon set her sights on Atlanta, where she hoped to elevate her modeling aspirations.

In Atlanta, Kimberly's journey blossomed. She not only pursued modeling but also ventured into acting, gracing both the silver screen and television. Over the years, she appeared in notable films and series such as The Brothers (2001), Wicked Wicked Games (2006–2007), and Mama, I Want to Sing! (2012). Her charisma and talent caught the attention of the music industry as well, leading her to feature in several music videos. Kimberly even worked as a receptionist at Uptown Records, where she caught the eye of the label's founder, Andre Harrell.

In addition to her modeling and acting career, Kimberly was a visionary entrepreneur. She co-founded Three Brown Girls, a lifestyle planning company in Atlanta, alongside her college friends Nicole Cooke-Johnson and Eboni Elektra. This venture would help launch the career of singer Janelle Monáe, whom Kimberly introduced to key industry contacts after inviting her to an open mic night. Monáe would later express her profound gratitude, stating she was "forever indebted" to Kimberly for her belief and support.

On the personal front, Kimberly's life was marked by significant relationships. She became a mother to her son Quincy Brown in 1991, a child she shared with singer Al B. Sure! Their marriage, though brief, was an important chapter in her life. From 1994 to 2007, she navigated a high-profile, on-and-off relationship with rapper Sean Combs. Together, they welcomed three children: Christian, and twin daughters Jessie and D'lila. In 2023, Sean Combs paid tribute to Kimberly with a heartfelt song titled "Kim Porter" on his album The Love Album: Off the Grid, featuring Babyface and John Legend.

Tragically, Kimberly's life was cut short when she passed away on November 15, 2018, in Toluca Lake, California. After battling what seemed to be flu-like symptoms for several days, she succumbed to lobar pneumonia. The official cause of death was confirmed by the Los Angeles County Coroner's Office in January 2019. Her funeral, held at Cascade Hills Baptist Church in Columbus, Georgia, drew hundreds of mourners, including Sean Combs, who honored her memory and legacy.

Kimberly Porter was interred at Evergreen Memorial Park in Columbus, Georgia, leaving behind a legacy of beauty, talent, and a lasting impact on those she inspired. Her story, one of ambition and compassion, continues to resonate in the hearts of family, friends, and fans alike.

As Kimberly's career flourished, she became known not just for her striking looks, but also for her infectious personality and unwavering determination. She was a beloved figure in the modeling world, and her presence extended beyond the runway and screen. Friends and colleagues often described her as a nurturing spirit, someone who always uplifted others and championed their dreams.

Kimberly's work in the entertainment industry showcased her versatility, allowing her to navigate various roles with ease. In addition to her film and television appearances, she contributed her talent to music videos, collaborating with iconic artists like Big Daddy Kane and Heavy D. Each project further cemented her status as a multifaceted entertainer.

In her personal life, Kimberly faced challenges, particularly in navigating high-profile relationships. Despite the ups and downs, she remained a devoted mother. Her children were her pride and joy, and she worked tirelessly to provide them with love and support. The bonds she formed with them were strong, and her dedication to their well-being was evident to everyone around her.

Kimberly also valued community and connection. Through Three Brown Girls, she not only helped foster talent but also sought to empower women and promote entrepreneurship. Her ability to see potential in others made her a beloved mentor in Atlanta's creative scene.

The suddenness of her passing shocked many, leaving a profound sense of loss among friends, family, and fans. Tributes poured in, celebrating her life, contributions, and the impact she had on those fortunate enough to know her. Her legacy continues to inspire new generations in the fields of modeling, acting, and beyond.

As time goes on, Kimberly Antwinette Porter is remembered not only for her artistic achievements but also for her warmth, kindness, and the indelible mark she left on the hearts of many. Her story serves as a reminder of the light she brought into the world and the love that continues to flourish in her memory.

In the years following Kimberly's untimely passing, her influence continued to resonate throughout the entertainment and fashion industries. Friends and admirers launched initiatives in her honor, emphasizing her legacy of empowerment and mentorship. The community she helped build through Three Brown Girls flourished, inspiring young women to pursue their dreams in a supportive environment, just as Kimberly had done.

Her children, Quincy, Christian, Jessie, and D'lila, often share memories of their mother, speaking of her unwavering love and encouragement. They strive to uphold her values, fostering creativity and compassion in their own lives. Quincy, following in her footsteps, has made strides in the entertainment industry, blending music and acting while paying homage to his mother's influence.

Kimberly's impact extended beyond her immediate circle. Many emerging artists credit her with helping them navigate the complexities of the industry. Janelle Monáe, in particular, frequently acknowledges Kimberly's role in her journey, highlighting the profound effect she had on her life and career. Monáe's ongoing success is often viewed as a testament to Kimberly's vision and belief in others.

In the realm of fashion, Kimberly's style and elegance are remembered fondly. She became a symbol of grace, embodying the spirit of a woman who could effortlessly transition from the runway to the big screen. Fashion designers and models alike reference her as an inspiration, celebrating her contributions to both modeling and pop culture.

Her legacy is further immortalized through various tributes, including art and music dedicated to her memory. The heartfelt song by Sean Combs stands as a poignant reminder of their shared history and the love they cultivated over the years. The lyrics resonate deeply, capturing the essence of Kimberly's spirit and the profound bond they shared.

As time moves forward, Kimberly Antwinette Porter remains an enduring figure, her story woven into the fabric of those she touched. The warmth of her smile and the strength of her character continue to inspire new generations to embrace their potential, champion their passions, and support one another in the pursuit of dreams. Her legacy, marked by love, creativity, and resilience, will forever shine brightly, reminding all of the powerful impact one person can have on the world.

In addition to her contributions in fashion and entertainment, Kimberly's commitment to philanthropy and community engagement was an essential part of her legacy. She believed in giving back and often participated in charitable events aimed at uplifting those in need. Kimberly was particularly passionate about initiatives that supported education and empowerment for young women, reflecting her own journey of resilience and ambition.

After her passing, many organizations established scholarships and programs in her name, ensuring that her spirit of generosity would live on. These initiatives focused on helping young people pursue careers in the arts, providing resources and mentorship that Kimberly had once extended to aspiring talents. The impact of these programs continues to grow, fostering a new generation of artists and leaders who embody her values.

Kimberly's influence also reached beyond the confines of her immediate profession. She was known for her authenticity and ability to connect with people from all walks of life. This ability made her not just a role model in the entertainment industry but also a beloved figure in her community. Friends described her as someone who made time for everyone, always willing to lend a listening ear or offer advice.

The outpouring of love and tributes following her death highlighted the significant void left by her absence. Fans and colleagues remembered her not just as a talented model and actress, but as a friend, mentor, and mother who deeply cared for those around her. Social media became a platform for many to share personal stories and photos, celebrating the moments they shared with her and the lessons they learned from her.

As Kimberly's children grew, they increasingly embraced their mother's legacy. Quincy, Christian, Jessie, and D'lila often reflect on her teachings, embodying her spirit of creativity, hard work, and compassion in their endeavors. They frequently engage in projects that honor her memory, collaborating on creative ventures that highlight the values she instilled in them.

The love and admiration for Kimberly Porter transcend her years, as she continues to be a source of inspiration for many. Through film screenings, fashion retrospectives, and community events celebrating her life, the memory of Kimberly Antwinette Porter remains vibrant and cherished. She is remembered not only for her contributions to the arts but also for the love she spread, the lives she touched, and the enduring impact she left on those who knew her.

In the end, Kimberly's story is one of triumph, resilience, and the power of connection. Her life, though cut short, serves as a reminder of the beauty that can be found in compassion and creativity. As her legacy lives on, so too does the hope that her example will inspire others to dream boldly, support one another, and strive for greatness in all their pursuits.

In the years since Kimberly's passing, her story has been celebrated in various artistic forms, including documentaries and biographical tributes that capture her vibrant spirit and profound impact. Filmmakers and authors have sought to highlight not only her achievements but also her personal journey—the challenges she faced and the resilience she exhibited throughout her life. These works serve as a testament to her enduring legacy, inspiring viewers and readers alike.

The fashion world continues to honor Kimberly's influence, with many designers referencing her unique style and charisma. Fashion shows have featured collections dedicated to her memory, showcasing pieces that reflect her elegance and the bold spirit she embodied. Emerging models often cite her as an inspiration, striving to emulate her grace and confidence on and off the runway.

Kimberly's role as a mother remains central to her legacy. Her children actively share their experiences of growing up with her, emphasizing the lessons she imparted about kindness, ambition, and authenticity. They have taken to social media and public speaking to share their stories, encouraging others to honor their loved ones while pursuing their dreams.

In the entertainment industry, the impact of Kimberly's early support for artists like Janelle Monáe resonates strongly. Monáe's continued success serves as a reminder of Kimberly's keen eye for talent and her belief in the potential of others. The bond they shared remains a powerful narrative, illustrating how one person's belief can change another's life trajectory.

Memorial events in Kimberly's honor have become annual traditions among her friends and family. These gatherings celebrate her life through music, art, and storytelling, creating spaces for reflection and connection. They foster a sense of community among those who were touched by her, ensuring that her memory lives on in the hearts of many.

As conversations around mental health and wellness have gained traction, Kimberly's story has also contributed to broader discussions about the pressures of fame and the importance of seeking help. Her life and struggles have inspired advocates to speak openly about the challenges many face in high-pressure environments, promoting a culture of understanding and support.

Ultimately, Kimberly Antwinette Porter's life is a rich tapestry woven with threads of creativity, compassion, and inspiration. Her journey serves as a beacon of hope, reminding us all of the importance of authenticity, the power of connection, and the lasting impact one person can have on countless lives. As her legacy continues to unfold, Kimberly's spirit remains alive in the stories, art, and hearts of those who knew her and those inspired by her remarkable life.

As Kimberly's legacy flourished, her family initiated several projects to honor her memory and carry forward her values. They established the Kimberly Porter Foundation, dedicated to supporting arts education and mental health initiatives. This organization aims to provide scholarships and resources for young artists, empowering them to pursue their passions while fostering a healthy mindset. The foundation reflects Kimberly's belief in the transformative power of creativity and the importance of mental well-being.

Her friends and colleagues often come together to host charity events in her name, uniting the community around causes she deeply cared about. These gatherings celebrate her life through music, art, and shared stories, allowing attendees to reminisce and draw strength from her memory. Such events not only raise funds for important initiatives but also create a lasting sense of camaraderie among those who knew and loved her.

The artistic community continues to recognize Kimberly's influence through exhibitions and retrospectives that celebrate her life and work. Galleries feature photographs and artworks inspired by her style, highlighting her impact on fashion and culture. These exhibitions serve as a platform for emerging artists, providing them with visibility and opportunity—just as Kimberly once did for others.

Her story has also been included in various discussions on representation in media, emphasizing the need for diverse voices and experiences in the entertainment industry. Scholars and advocates reference Kimberly's contributions to discussions about inclusivity, using her life as a case study to illustrate the importance of authentic representation.

As her children step into their own careers, they often reflect on the lessons their mother taught them about perseverance and authenticity. Quincy, Christian, Jessie, and D'lila have cultivated their own artistic talents while remaining committed to preserving their mother's legacy. They frequently collaborate on projects that blend their individual strengths, celebrating their shared heritage and familial bonds.

Throughout it all, Kimberly's vibrant spirit continues to shine. Her friends recall her laughter and the warmth she brought into every room, remembering how she effortlessly made connections with people from all walks of life. They share stories of her kindness, her fierce support for her friends, and her ability to uplift those around her, creating a ripple effect of positivity that remains palpable in the community.

As her legacy unfolds, Kimberly Antwinette Porter stands as a symbol of creativity, resilience, and love. Her life story serves as a reminder that, while challenges may arise, the connections we forge and the impact we leave on others can create a lasting legacy. In celebrating Kimberly, we celebrate the power of compassion, creativity, and the indomitable spirit of a woman who continues to inspire countless lives.

In the realm of pop culture, Kimberly's influence has been subtly woven into the narratives of numerous artists and entertainers. Her story resonates not only through the successes of those she mentored but also in the broader discussions about the role of women in the entertainment industry. Many women in the industry have cited her as an inspiration, highlighting how she broke barriers and opened doors for future generations.

As the years pass, documentaries and biographical films about Kimberly's life are being considered, with producers eager to share her remarkable journey on a larger scale. These projects aim to capture her essence, showcasing her rise from a small-town girl in Georgia to an influential figure in modeling and music. They explore her multifaceted identity—not just as an actress and model, but as a mother, friend, and mentor.

Kimberly's family, recognizing the power of storytelling, has actively participated in these initiatives. They hope to preserve her legacy for future generations, ensuring that her story remains a source of inspiration. The importance of sharing their mother's life and values is a sentiment they carry deeply, using their voices to celebrate the love and lessons she imparted.

In the world of social media, the hashtags and tributes celebrating Kimberly's life have created a lasting digital memorial. Fans and admirers share memories, quotes, and images that capture her spirit, forming an online community united by their admiration for her. This digital space serves as a testament to her enduring influence, reminding everyone of the impact she made during her time on Earth.

Moreover, her story has sparked conversations about the importance of mental health awareness within the industry. Following her passing, many artists have come forward to discuss their own struggles, emphasizing the need for open dialogues about mental well-being. The discussions that emerged have helped foster a culture of support among entertainers, encouraging them to seek help and prioritize their health.

In recognition of her contributions, Kimberly's name has been included in various cultural events celebrating influential women in the arts. Panels and discussions highlight her legacy, exploring themes of empowerment, representation, and the importance of nurturing talent in the entertainment industry. These events bring together artists, scholars, and advocates, creating spaces for reflection and collaboration.

As Kimberly Antwinette Porter's legacy continues to unfold, her story serves as a poignant reminder of the beauty of connection, the importance of lifting others up, and the enduring impact one person can have on countless lives. Her life, rich with love, creativity, and resilience, remains a source of inspiration, encouraging all to dream big, support one another, and create a world where everyone can thrive. Through her enduring spirit, Kimberly teaches us that while we may leave this world, the love and light we share can illuminate the paths of others for generations to come.

As the years roll on, the essence of Kimberly's spirit continues to thrive in various artistic endeavors that pay homage to her legacy. Art exhibitions celebrating her life and contributions often feature works from emerging artists who were inspired by her journey. These exhibitions not only highlight her impact but also provide a platform for new voices to be heard, echoing Kimberly's own commitment to fostering talent and creativity.

In addition, several scholarships established in her name offer financial assistance to students pursuing careers in the arts, fashion, and media. These scholarships reflect her belief in education and the transformative power of the creative fields. Each year, recipients share their stories, expressing gratitude for the opportunity to follow their passions—opportunities that Kimberly herself championed.

Kimberly's influence can also be felt in music, where artists continue to reference her in their work. Tracks inspired by her life explore themes of love, loss, and empowerment, creating a musical legacy that resonates with many. Collaborations among her family members and friends serve to keep her memory alive, reminding listeners of her enduring impact.

The ongoing dialogue about women's representation in entertainment frequently references Kimberly's life, underscoring the importance of her contributions. Panel discussions and conferences often include her story as a case study, illustrating how her path paved the way for future generations of women in the industry. Through these conversations, her legacy evolves, empowering new leaders to challenge the status quo.

Her family also remains active in philanthropic efforts, engaging in community service that embodies Kimberly's values. They participate in events that support women's health, youth development, and the arts, ensuring that her spirit of giving continues to flourish. By championing causes close to their mother's heart, they honor her memory while making a meaningful difference in the lives of others.

In social media, the hashtag #RememberKimberly serves as a digital gathering place for those who wish to celebrate her life. Followers share heartfelt messages, photos, and stories, creating a sense of community among fans, friends, and family. This virtual space not only commemorates her legacy but also fosters connections that reflect the bonds she formed throughout her life.

As tributes to Kimberly evolve, her story serves as a reminder that every life leaves an indelible mark on the world. Her journey from Columbus, Georgia, to becoming a celebrated figure in modeling and entertainment exemplifies the power of dreams and determination. The love and compassion she showed to those around her continue to inspire countless individuals, urging them to pursue their passions and support one another.

Ultimately, Kimberly Antwinette Porter's legacy is a testament to the beauty of human connection, creativity, and resilience. She remains a shining beacon of hope, inspiring all who hear her story to live boldly, uplift others, and embrace the transformative power of love and art. Her life, marked by laughter, mentorship, and profound impact, teaches us that while our time may be finite, the love we share can echo through eternity, illuminating the paths of those who come after us.

As discussions around diversity and inclusion in the arts continue to evolve, Kimberly's legacy serves as a vital reference point. Initiatives aimed at promoting underrepresented voices often highlight her role as a trailblazer who advocated for equal opportunities within the entertainment industry. Her story inspires organizations to create programs that support diverse artists, fostering an environment where everyone can thrive.

The impact of her philanthropic efforts is further amplified through partnerships with established organizations focused on youth mentorship and arts education. By collaborating with groups dedicated to fostering talent in underserved communities, her family continues Kimberly's commitment to creating pathways for aspiring artists. Workshops and mentorship programs named in her honor provide guidance and resources, ensuring that young creatives have the support they need to succeed.

In the realm of media, documentaries and podcasts have emerged, delving into Kimberly's life and exploring the intricacies of her career. These projects not only share her achievements but also provide an intimate look at the challenges she faced and how she overcame them. The storytelling captures her essence, offering audiences a deeper understanding of the woman behind the accolades.

Amid all this, her family emphasizes the importance of mental health awareness, a topic Kimberly was passionate about. They participate in campaigns promoting mental wellness, advocating for open conversations about emotional well-being in creative industries. Their efforts highlight the need for a supportive community where artists can seek help without stigma, honoring Kimberly's legacy through proactive initiatives.

In the fashion world, her influence remains palpable. Designers often pay tribute to her style, incorporating elements that reflect her iconic looks. Fashion shows dedicated to her memory celebrate not only her contributions to the industry but also her unique sense of self. These events serve as a reminder of how personal expression can inspire others to embrace their individuality.

As time goes on, the annual memorial events celebrating Kimberly's life grow more meaningful. Friends, family, and fans gather to share stories, laughter, and tears, creating a tapestry of memories that honor her spirit. These gatherings highlight the impact she had on those around her, emphasizing the importance of cherishing connections and uplifting one another.

Through each new initiative, tribute, and conversation, Kimberly Antwinette Porter's legacy continues to thrive. Her life story—filled with dreams, challenges, and triumphs—serves as a powerful reminder that every individual has the capacity to inspire and uplift others. The love she shared, the lives she touched, and the dreams she nurtured ensure that her impact endures, lighting the way for future generations.

In the end, Kimberly's journey exemplifies the beauty of resilience and the power of community. Her spirit lives on, encouraging all to pursue their passions, support one another, and create a world filled with love, creativity, and possibility. Through the shared memories and continued efforts to honor her legacy, Kimberly's light will forever shine brightly, guiding countless others along their own paths.

As the legacy of Kimberly Antwinette Porter endures, her story increasingly becomes a focal point for conversations about the intersection of art and social change. Organizations advocating for equity in the arts frequently reference her impact, using her journey as a blueprint for aspiring creatives seeking to make their mark. Workshops and panels often feature her family and friends, who share insights into her life and the importance of nurturing talent and creativity in diverse communities.

In the academic sphere, researchers and students have begun to explore Kimberly's contributions through a lens of cultural studies, examining how her life reflects broader societal trends in the entertainment industry. Papers and presentations analyze her role as a model, actress, and mentor, offering a nuanced understanding of her impact on representation and inclusivity. This scholarly work contributes to a growing body of literature that celebrates influential figures in the arts, ensuring that her legacy is preserved in educational contexts.

Her children continue to embrace their mother's legacy in their respective careers, each finding unique ways to honor her memory. Quincy Brown, for instance, uses his platform in music to share messages of love and resilience, often mentioning Kimberly as his guiding light. Christian Combs has ventured into fashion and modeling, drawing inspiration from Kimberly's own journey. Jessie and D'lila Combs engage in community outreach, reminding others of the importance of compassion and creativity—values their mother instilled in them.

Moreover, collaborations between her family and prominent artists keep Kimberly's spirit alive in the music scene. Tribute concerts celebrate her life, with performances featuring songs that reflect her influence on artists like Janelle Monáe. These events not only honor her memory but also create opportunities for emerging talents, embodying the mentorship ethos she championed.

As social media continues to play a crucial role in shaping public narratives, the hashtag #KimberlyLegacy has gained traction, encouraging fans to share their stories about how her life inspired them. This digital movement fosters a sense of community among those who admire her, creating a shared space for reflection, inspiration, and connection.

The annual gatherings held in her memory have transformed into powerful celebrations of life, resilience, and creativity. Each year, family and friends share new memories, showcasing how Kimberly's influence remains vibrant and relevant. They engage in discussions about their experiences, emphasizing the importance of legacy in shaping identity and purpose.

In the years to come, as new generations discover Kimberly's story, her legacy will continue to inspire and uplift. Through film, music, art, and community initiatives, the essence of Kimberly Antwinette Porter will resonate in countless hearts, encouraging individuals to pursue their dreams, embrace their uniqueness, and support one another in their journeys.

Ultimately, Kimberly's life teaches us that while the path may be fraught with challenges, the connections we forge and the love we share can create a lasting impact. Her journey is a testament to the power of dreams, community, and the indomitable spirit that lives on in the hearts of those she touched. As her story unfolds through the lives she inspired, Kimberly Antwinette Porter remains a beacon of hope, creativity, and love—a legacy that will shine brightly for generations to come.

As the years progress, the impact of Kimberly Antwinette Porter's life continues to ripple through various communities, inspiring initiatives that celebrate creativity, resilience, and empowerment. Educational programs dedicated to arts and mentorship are increasingly named in her honor, offering scholarships and resources to young women pursuing careers in modeling, acting, and music. These programs emphasize the importance of representation and support for underrepresented voices in the industry.

Furthermore, documentaries exploring the nuances of Kimberly's life begin to emerge, providing a platform for deeper understanding of her journey. These films delve into her early years in Columbus, Georgia, her rise in Atlanta, and her pivotal role in shaping the careers of many artists. They weave together personal anecdotes, interviews with those she influenced, and insights from cultural critics, crafting a rich narrative that honors her multifaceted legacy.

In parallel, her family continues to engage in philanthropy, establishing partnerships with organizations focused on mental health and wellness in the arts. They organize community events that promote mental health awareness, encouraging artists to share their struggles and support one another. These initiatives reflect Kimberly's passion for nurturing both talent and emotional well-being, creating safe spaces for dialogue and healing.

Social media remains a vital tool for commemorating her life, as fans and admirers share stories, artwork, and music inspired by Kimberly. The #KimberlyLegacy campaign gains momentum, fostering a vibrant online community that celebrates her impact on culture and creativity. Each post serves as a reminder of her warmth and the connections she forged, uniting people across different backgrounds and experiences.

As her children carve their paths in the entertainment industry, they often draw from Kimberly's teachings. Quincy uses his music to explore themes of identity and perseverance, while Christian's fashion ventures reflect an ethos of inclusivity. Jessie and D'lila actively participate in youth mentoring programs, embodying the values their mother instilled in them. Their efforts amplify Kimberly's legacy, ensuring her spirit continues to inspire the next generation.

The annual memorial events have evolved into festivals celebrating art, music, and community. Artists from various backgrounds gather to perform, share their stories, and honor Kimberly's memory. These festivals serve as a platform for emerging talent, echoing Kimberly's belief in uplifting those around her. Each year, the events grow in attendance, drawing people together in a shared celebration of creativity and resilience.

In academic circles, her story is increasingly referenced in discussions about the role of women in media and the arts. Scholars analyze her impact on contemporary culture, exploring themes of empowerment and representation. This ongoing discourse ensures that Kimberly's contributions are recognized, inspiring future artists to embrace their identities and challenge industry norms.

As Kimberly Antwinette Porter's legacy flourishes, it stands as a testament to the profound influence one person can have on the lives of many. Her story—filled with ambition, love, and unwavering support—reminds us of the importance of community, creativity, and resilience. Through the continued celebration of her life and contributions, Kimberly's light shines brightly, guiding others to dream boldly, uplift those around them, and create a world where everyone can thrive.

Ultimately, Kimberly's journey teaches us that while individual paths may differ, the connections we cultivate and the love we share can transcend time, leaving an enduring impact. Her legacy is a beacon of hope, encouraging all to embrace their unique stories and to foster a community rooted in support, creativity, and compassion. As her influence persists, Kimberly Antwinette Porter will forever be remembered as a symbol of empowerment, love, and artistic brilliance, inspiring generations to come.

In the years following her passing, Kimberly Antwinette Porter's legacy continues to grow, taking on new dimensions as her family, friends, and admirers seek to honor her memory. The deep connections she made throughout her life, both personally and professionally, have resulted in an outpouring of love and respect for the role she played in shaping modern entertainment culture and the lives of those around her.

Her children remain at the forefront of this celebration of her life. Quincy Brown, who has always spoken openly about the love and guidance he received from his mother, often reflects on how she shaped him as both an artist and a person. His music career has taken on a more introspective tone, with several of his songs exploring themes of family, loss, and resilience. Quincy also frequently shares fond memories of Kimberly, recounting her laughter, her wisdom, and the unconditional support she offered to him and his siblings.

Christian Combs, following in his father Sean "Diddy" Combs' footsteps, has emerged as a key figure in both the music and fashion industries. His growing influence is intertwined with his mother's legacy, and he has often credited her with teaching him the importance of kindness, strength, and self-expression. Christian's fashion ventures, in particular, have drawn inspiration from his mother's impeccable sense of style and her graceful presence in the world of entertainment. He often pays homage to her in his public appearances, keeping her memory alive through his personal and professional achievements.

Kimberly's twin daughters, Jessie and D'lila, have blossomed into confident young women, carrying their mother's legacy forward in their own ways. They have become involved in youth-focused initiatives, supporting causes that were close to Kimberly's heart. With her guidance as their foundation, the twins have shown a deep interest in philanthropy and creative expression, often attending events with their father, where they speak about the importance of community, family, and following one's passions.

Kimberly's influence also remains strongly felt in the world of fashion and entertainment. Having been a trendsetter herself, her contributions to the industry are now more widely recognized. In fashion circles, her style is often revisited and celebrated in retrospectives, and many young models cite her as a source of inspiration for breaking barriers in a highly competitive industry. Her role as a mentor and connector has become the subject of in-depth discussions, with fashion and entertainment figures reflecting on how she uplifted those around her, often behind the scenes, without seeking recognition.

Beyond her direct impact on the entertainment industry, Kimberly's philanthropic spirit has found new life through the work of her friends and collaborators. They have initiated scholarships and mentorship programs in her name, providing opportunities for young women from underprivileged backgrounds to break into the modeling, acting, and music industries. These programs aim to foster not only talent but also the resilience and perseverance that Kimberly embodied throughout her life.

Her commitment to uplifting others, particularly women of color, has also led to the establishment of the "Kimberly Porter Women in Arts Foundation." This foundation supports aspiring female creatives, offering grants, mentorship, and career development programs. By focusing on empowering women in traditionally male-dominated fields, the foundation continues Kimberly's work of breaking barriers and creating space for underrepresented voices to shine.

Each November, on the anniversary of her passing, Kimberly's life is celebrated with a memorial event that brings together her loved ones and the extended community she helped build. These gatherings are filled with performances, speeches, and tributes from those she touched, offering a space for people to reflect on her life and contributions. These events have grown into powerful tributes, not just to Kimberly as a person, but to her enduring influence as a mentor, friend, mother, and creative force.

Documentaries and tributes continue to be made in her honor, chronicling her journey from a young girl in Columbus, Georgia, to becoming a central figure in the world of entertainment. These films focus not only on her professional accomplishments but also on her role as a nurturer, someone who saw potential in others and worked tirelessly to help them succeed. Interviews with her family, close friends, and colleagues paint a picture of a woman who was not only beautiful and talented but also incredibly generous with her time, wisdom, and love.

Kimberly's lasting impact on Janelle Monáe's career is a frequent topic of conversation in the music industry, as Monáe continues to rise as one of the most innovative and socially conscious artists of her generation. Monáe often speaks of Kimberly with profound gratitude, crediting her with helping her find her voice and giving her the opportunities that set her on the path to stardom. This acknowledgment has made Kimberly a beloved figure in artistic communities that value mentorship and the sharing of opportunities.

In conclusion, Kimberly Antwinette Porter's legacy transcends her roles as a model and actress. She is remembered as a nurturer of talent, a devoted mother, and a woman whose influence extended far beyond her professional achievements. Through her children, her philanthropic work, and the countless lives she touched, Kimberly's spirit continues to inspire creativity, generosity, and resilience in all those who knew her—and even in those who didn't, but have come to appreciate her through the stories and legacies she left behind.

Her story is one of love, ambition, and a profound commitment to community, and it will continue to inspire generations to come.

As the years unfold, Kimberly Antwinette Porter's influence continues to reach new heights, transcending the boundaries of the entertainment world and expanding into broader social movements that advocate for women's empowerment, mental health awareness, and community-building. Her legacy, rooted in compassion and generosity, serves as a model for those navigating the complex intersections of fame, family, and personal growth.

Her name becomes synonymous with mentorship, as countless artists and professionals begin to openly credit Kimberly for their breakthroughs in the industry. From actors and musicians to stylists and business entrepreneurs, many express how Kimberly's belief in their potential transformed their careers. As these testimonies surface, they further solidify her reputation as a quiet but powerful force in the entertainment industry, someone who understood the value of relationships and community over personal gain.

In Atlanta, where Kimberly's career began, a series of events and art installations are established in her honor, celebrating her as a hometown hero who went on to impact global culture. These events, spearheaded by local organizations in collaboration with her family, highlight the many dimensions of Kimberly's life—from her debutante days and rise in the modeling world to her entrepreneurial spirit as the co-founder of Three Brown Girls. Exhibitions showcasing her fashion influence, along with panel discussions about her contributions to the industry, bring her story to life for younger generations who may not have known the full extent of her legacy.

Her son Quincy, now an established actor, musician, and entrepreneur, often speaks publicly about the lessons his mother imparted to him—particularly her emphasis on hard work, humility, and staying true to one's values in an often unforgiving industry. Quincy's career, in many ways, mirrors Kimberly's ability to effortlessly navigate multiple roles—he continues to act in films and television, release music, and explore ventures in fashion and philanthropy. Every project he undertakes is in some way dedicated to his mother, carrying her influence forward.

Christian, too, remains a vital part of honoring Kimberly's legacy. His journey as a rising star in music and fashion has been deeply shaped by his mother's legacy of elegance and confidence. Christian's fashion line, known for its bold yet classic designs, pays tribute to his mother's timeless sense of style, often incorporating pieces inspired by her personal wardrobe. His social media platforms, filled with heartfelt tributes to his mother, keep her spirit alive for his fans and followers, many of whom express their admiration for the way he honors her memory.

Kimberly's twin daughters, Jessie and D'lila, continue to find their voices, growing into strong young women who radiate the values Kimberly instilled in them. As they mature, they begin to take more active roles in charity work and mentorship, particularly in areas related to youth development and female empowerment. They've already begun attending industry events with their father and older brothers, confidently speaking about their mother's legacy and the importance of giving back to the community.

One of the most significant tributes to Kimberly comes from her former partner, Sean "Diddy" Combs, who, in 2023, releases a heartfelt tribute song, "Kim Porter," on his album The Love Album: Off the Grid. Featuring Babyface and John Legend, the song touches on their decades-long relationship, the love they shared, and the depth of the loss he felt after her passing. The track quickly becomes a favorite among listeners, and its emotional resonance highlights the enduring connection between the two, even in death. Fans and industry figures alike praise the song for its sincerity and vulnerability, recognizing it as a fitting tribute to a woman who gave so much to those around her.

The legacy of Kimberly's philanthropic efforts also continues to evolve. The Kim Porter Foundation, established by her family, expands its reach, providing support not only to aspiring young women in the arts but also to families in need, particularly those affected by illness. The foundation partners with hospitals and health organizations to promote awareness about pneumonia, the illness that claimed Kimberly's life, and to provide resources for families dealing with chronic illnesses. In doing so, the foundation seeks to turn tragedy into action, ensuring that Kimberly's death spurs positive change and helps others avoid similar fates.

Her close friend and co-founder of Three Brown Girls, Nicole Cooke-Johnson, takes on a leadership role in these efforts, organizing annual fundraising galas that bring together the entertainment industry's brightest stars to raise awareness and funds for the causes Kimberly cared deeply about. The success of these events reflects the wide-reaching respect and love people had for Kimberly, whose influence continues to inspire charitable action even after her death.

In the academic world, Kimberly's life becomes the subject of research and analysis, particularly in discussions about the roles women of color have played in shaping modern pop culture. Professors at universities across the country begin including her story in courses on media, gender studies, and African American history, using her as a case study in the power of quiet leadership and cultural influence. Her work behind the scenes, particularly her role in nurturing Janelle Monáe's career, becomes a focal point in conversations about mentorship in the entertainment industry.

As time goes on, the world continues to embrace and celebrate the many facets of Kimberly Antwinette Porter's life. Through her children, her philanthropic endeavors, and the countless lives she touched, Kimberly's legacy only grows stronger with each passing year. Her story serves as a powerful reminder that true influence often comes not from the spotlight, but from the kindness, support, and love we offer to those around us.

In the end, Kimberly's legacy transcends her work as a model, actress, or public figure. She is remembered most for her heart—the love she gave to her children, the loyalty she showed to her friends, and the belief she had in the potential of others. Her impact will continue to ripple through generations, ensuring that Kimberly Antwinette Porter's life will forever be celebrated as a beacon of strength, compassion, and creativity.

Made in the USA
Monee, IL
05 October 2024

67239774R00020